TO
PROTECT
AND
SERVE

ARLENE ALMA POHL

ISBN 978-1-0980-8738-8 (paperback)
ISBN 978-1-0980-8740-1 (hardcover)
ISBN 978-1-0980-8739-5 (digital)

Christian Faith Publishing, Inc.
832 Park Avenue
Meadville, PA 16335
www.christianfaithpublishing.com

Printed in the United States of America

Contents

Tribute

To all law enforcement officers'
unwavering dedication to their
communities. God bless these
peacemakers who God has commanded to
watch over his people, the officers God
has commanded to uphold justice and
peace. Please recognize these officers
that obey God to do his will to protect
his sheep and strive for his almighty
justice.

Police

'Ministers serving as an agent for God in carrying out specific duties.'

P: POLISHED (In the representation of his department) Refined, Cultured & Flawless

O: OBLIGATED (To assure you of your safety) Constrained by a legal tie, Indebted

L: LICENSED (To police your community) Legal permission, Latitude of action

I: INITIATIVE (To serve and protect your community) Determination

C: CORDIAL (In the handling of calls of service) Fervent, Sincere, Stimulating

E: EQUAL (To the community's citizens) Identical in value, Impartial, Adequate

Strong and Bold...Blue

God has placed within your reach, a comfort to your soul. It's
    not some wealth nor silver, and certainly not of gold.
It is not something you dream of, it's not something you hold,
    it's a gift of love he gave to us, it's something strong and
    bold.
We've looked, we've searched, we've wandered far and near,
    wondering where our help comes from, but that help is
    very near.
Do not feel alone, do not feel afraid, God has you in his hands.
    He gave an assignment to the one in blue, to take care of
    you in his plans.
The one in blue is strong and bold, it's the comfort God has
    given,
Take heed and know you're in God's love, as the one in
    blue's...God-driven.

A prayer by Saint Teresa of Avila

Let nothing disturb you,
Nothing frighten you,
All things are passing,
God never changes,
Patient endurance attains all things,
Whoever possesses God is wanting in nothing:
God alone suffices.

9 ～ TO PROTECT AND SERVE

Blessed are the peacemakers, for they
shall be called sons of God.

—Matthew 5:9

Support

Please support all Law Enforcement Officers:
They are
Courageous
Ministers
Unwavering
Dedicated
Persevering
Equal
Patient
Fervent
Protecting
Strong
Bold
Selected
Sincere
Compassionate
Caring
Flexible
Heroic
Peacemaking
Thank you for praying for all law
enforcement officers—they deserve and need
our prayers every day.

Selective Few

It's a very special person,
God has chosen to,
Watch over all his sheep,
Who are scared and feeling blue.
God has selected several,
To protect and fervently serve,
The communities of his citizens,
To help cure all their fear.
He has chosen them with care,
Accepts only the best,
That follows not just his Word,
But those who serve with zest.
It takes a special person,
That serves our God above,
Who is selected with such care,
A desirer of God's love.
They strive to do God's work,
Those who succeed are few,
They love our Lord with all their heart,
And hatred they do not brood.

True Blue Hero

True Blue Hero,
How I pray for you,
You have no clue what call is next,
I always pray for you...
True Blue Hero,
You are so brave to me,
You do your work so wonderfully well,
Which people seldom see...
True Blue Hero,
Blessed with dignity,
Filled with strength from God above,
Gifted by Deity...
True Blue Hero,
You're selfless and you're kind,
Thank you for watching over me,
It's their wrong-doing that you bind.

Key

It may appear he's trembling, or retreating
Over here,
It may seem like he's ambling or kowtowing
Over there.
Friend, these notions that you conjure,
Are very incorrect,
Let me tell you a bit about him,
It's him you won't reject.
This K-9's full of tenacity and also
Readiness,
He's active and he's cautious, and working
With redress.
He is the key, and this is why,
His actions convey an officer, and this K-9
Will not lie.
This K-9 that you wonder 'bout,
Is a leader and a pro,
He's the one that will track your loved one,
In a place you dare not go.
God bless our K-9 Officers,
They will go anywhere,
To find your lost treasure safely,
In places you're unaware.

True Blue...
Sheepdog

I have a favorite sheepdog, who lives not far away,
I know that I'm in safety, his vigilance does not sway.
He guards his home and family,
His city and partners too,
Now you know him, don't you?
Of course, it's True Blue.
True to society, true to his wife and all those he meets,
True to his K-9 and his own courageous life.
If you do not know him yet,
You will someday see,
That this True Blue's a blessing,
To all of you and me.
You will surely know him,
By the way he stands, and walks,
With confidence and presence,
He is one that never balks.
He's positive and strong,
A never wavering soul,
He keeps all in perspective,
Persevering to his goal.
His goal's an unprecedented excellence,
One you don't often meet,
If you're wondering where your warrior's at,
This officer is the one you should meet.
He won't let you down,
Come to him wolf or sheep,

He's always on a forthright path,
It's your safety he will keep.
God bless this True Blue warrior,
Who sifts through mire and muck,
He comes through with rainbow colors,
Which is not attained through luck.
This blessed assignment of this cop,
Is from our God above,
Our God who made this cop courageous,
Is from God's abundant love.

Heavenly Father

Heavenly father,
I come to you with a fervent heart, with a
love for you that continues to grow and
believe in you.
I come to ask you for your continual
protection upon our law enforcement
officers. Help them to use your wisdom
and your judgment.
Please keep them safe, healthy, alive and
well. Protect them Lord from evil.
Please watch over them and please keep
all obstacles to their safety, away from
them. Please be our officers'
guide, protector, and leader.
I ask this in Your name, Lord. Amen.

Dear God,

Please bless our law enforcement officers.
In Jesus name I pray.
Amen.

Submission of Governing Authorities

Let everyone be subject to the governing authorities, for there is not authority except that which God has established. The authorities that exist have been established by God. Consequently, whoever rebels against the authority is rebelling against what God has instituted, and those who will do so bring judgment on themselves. For rulers hold no terror for those who do right, but for those who do wrong. Do you want to be free from fear of the one in authority? Then do what is right and you will be commended. For the one in authority is God's servant for your good. But if you do wrong, be afraid, for rulers do not bear the sword for no reason. They are God's servants, agents of wrath to bring punishment on the wrongdoer. Therefore, it is necessary to submit to the authorities, not only because of possible punishment but also as a matter of conscience.

—Romans 13:1–5

Yes, Blue Lives Do Matter...

You may not admit that now,
but as time goes on and you get stuck,
you realize a moment of wow…
Because that LEO has SWORN,
to keep you free from harm,
he puts himself behind you,
because his OATH is
what is worn.
Yes, Blue Lives Do Matter

Restorers
of Justice

Law Enforcement Officers
Are restorers of Justice...
Are those individuals who shine Christ's light. These chosen
few are individuals who are sworn in. Take that oath to
protect and serve...and in that oath, they make a decision to
NOT WAVER.

Those Law Enforcement Officers...

They are the best of the best, they are few and far between,
They make a choice to protect you, there's no right in saying
  they're mean.
They chose this field to serve, to protect us all from harm,
To always keep your loved ones safe and keep the needy warm.

Heavenly Father (K-9s)

HEAVENLY FATHER,

Let us never forget to pray for the K-9 Officers in all law enforcement agencies. They never hesitate to protect their partners.

We pray that you, Father God, continue to keep all K-9s safe and healthy as they willingly and happily protect their partners, their communities, and their agencies.

Thank you God, for your creation of K-9s and their innate desire to keep us all safe.

Amen.

IMG_4920.JPG

Matthew 18:20

*"…for where two or three are gathered in my name, there am
I in their midst…"*

My dear brothers and sisters in Christ, let us pray
together for those people who are not in support of Law
enforcement. Let us pray that they come to love
wisdom for the Lord. God's word proclaims,
'For the Lord giveth wisdom: out of his mouth cometh
knowledge and understanding. He layeth up sound
wisdom for the righteous, he is a buckler to them that
walk uprightly. He keepeth the paths of judgment and
preserveth the way of his saints. Then shalt thou
understand righteousness, judgment, equity and
every good path.
When wisdom entereth into thine heart, and
knowledge is pleasant unto thy soul:
discretion shall preserve thee,
understanding shall keep thee,
to deliver thee from the way of the evil man,
from the man that speaketh forward things,
who leave the paths of uprightness,
to walk in the ways of darkness, who rejoice to do evil
and delight in the forwardness of the wicked,

whose ways are crooked and they forward in their paths.'

Heavenly Father, we come in your name asking you to heal the broken hearted who turn to evil ways, in Jesus's name, Amen.

I Proudly Back the Blue

I am a mother who backs the Blue, my continuous prayers are
for all those in Blue.
My arms lifted upward, all day and all night, Oh dear God I beg
you, make people live right.
Make evil flee Lord, please bring this world peace, convert the
wrong-doers Lord, please make this crime cease.

A Parent's Child—A Police Officer

You will see him taking pictures,
You will see him making stops,
He gives the tourist directions,
It's all about being a cop...
A thin blue line he contends with,
Day and night and in between,
He's chastised, name called, laughed at,
But assuredly, he gleams...
Running hot, chasing runners,
Diligently doing his work,
Don't test him my friend,
He's in control,
It won't pay being a jerk...
Respect the man in blue,
He's at your beck and call,
He's here to keep you safe,
When you're up against a wall...
Mess not with his partners,
He's always got their back,
It's wisest to obey them,
They are confident pack...
Be kind my friend to the man in blue,
He may not be someone you know,

But he may be the one to save your life,
Please ask me how I know…
I know he will protect you,
I know him very well,
It's my own son who I speak of here,
I have this truth to tell.

An Officer's Wife...

Is she who sees him get ready for work, watching as he pulls away, never knowing what this shift will bring, accepting come what may...

Her hug and kiss will sustain him, reminding him he's cared for, he has her love to return to, one another those two are made for...

She will pray for him that daily prayer, "Dear God, please keep him safe." It's true to say that daily prayer, increases her strength and faith.

She knows that our God hears her, her soul so filled with faith, it's not just this one time prayer this shift, its many prayers she creates.

She loves her husband dearly and he cares so much for her, she can't wait till he comes home, he will hug her to be sure.

Besides her very own work to do, there's a beautiful daughter too, together they clean, they cook, and bake and wait for their man in blue.

It's a lovely day and a happy time when the man in blue comes home, there's been some worry and lots of prayers... thank God that man came home.

Steadily, Readily

...Is the path he always goes, what he may be called to do today, you, me, nor he, ever knows...His uniform always pressed, his polished boots do sheen, his tactical gear is organized, his demeanor always beams...The unknown is a weary place, the unknown so unclear, keep this peacemaker in your prayers, it's God's image which he mirrors.

Prayer to Saint Michael by Pope Leo XIII

Saint Michael the Archangel, defend us in battle, be our protection
against the wickedness and snares of the devil.
May God rebuke him, we humbly pray, and do thou oh prince of
the heavenly host, by the power of God, thrust into hell Satan, and
all the evil spirits who prowl about the world, seeking the ruin of
souls.
Amen.

Law Enforcement Officers' Virtues

He does withstand adversity
He is blessed with courage and strength
He has emotional power and the
Gift of follow through...
He can truthfully claim habitual moderation
Living with a great restraint
Which is always renewed...
He lives his life with discipline
Using good judgment
Vigilance and cautiousness...
Our Law Enforcement Officers are blessed by the Holy Spirit
    with these
Virtues of
Fortitude...Temperance...Prudence
Thank you, God, for preparing them for the battlefield. Amen

Heavenly Father (Fallen Blue)

Our faithful fallen officers never did waver.
When they made their justice-fighting
presence at the scene of that crime, they gave
their lives.
It's in that fighting of that crime, protecting
all society from evil, that they made the
ultimate sacrifice.
To those of you who have lost a loved LEO, I
assure you that your LEO is prayed for,
thanked, and cherished.

Heavenly Father, I ask you to take our faithful, courageous, fallen officers to your heavenly streets of joy, to your waters of peace, and to your presence of righteousness and goodness. In Jesus's name I pray, Amen. From the deepest recesses of my soul, I honor the fallen... you who are our warriors, patriots, and true blue heroes.

I thank you for your brave and selfless service; and part of us dies when you gave all. Your blue family has the watch and may God grant you eternal rest with him. My fallen friends, as a mother of the blue, I proudly back the blue, and I thank you. A final salute. You are now 10–7 in the arms of our Heavenly Father, receiving your eternal reward for the work you have done in this battlefield. Rest in peace and thank you for your service.

Peacemakers

Dear God,

Please protect your peacemakers.

This commemorative is a reminder to all who have lost
a loved one in the line of duty. Know that your support,
love, and prayers for the officers were not in vain.

Also, this commemorative is for families who continue
to pray to God for his care over your loved ones as
they continue to provide safety to our world.

May God bless the sheepdogs.

May God bless our law enforcement officers as they
provide protection to our communities and put us first.

Thank You, God, for the officers' service.

Dispatch: 217

Dispatch: 217
217: 217: Received a call from the complainant at the address you just cleared. Complainant wanted to thank you for your professionalism and your compassion while at their home where their 16-year old son threatened to commit suicide. They wanted to share how kind and sincere you were, that your demeanor and knowledge has given their family much needed hope for the upcoming precarious days ahead.
217: 10-4

Well done, good and faithful servant. You have been faithful.

—Matthew 25:21

Police Lives Matter

Police lives matter. In the name of Jesus Christ. Amen.